HORRIBLE HISTORIES

...rry Deary illustrated by **Martin Brown**

SCHOLASTIC

Published in the UK by Scholastic Children's Books, 2020
Euston House, 24 Eversholt Street, London, NW1 1DB, UK
A division of Scholastic Limited

London ~ New York ~ Toronto ~ Sydney ~ Auckland
Mexico City ~ New Delhi ~ Hong Kong

SCHOLASTIC and associated logos are trademarks and/or
registered trademarks of Scholastic Inc.

Text © Terry Deary, 2020
Cover illustration © Martin Brown, 2020; line and colour by Rob Davis
Inside illustrations © Martin Brown, 2020

ISBN 978 1407 19679 4

A CIP catalogue record for this book is available from the British Library.

Printed and bound in the UK by CPI Group (UK) Ltd, Croydon, CRO 4YY

Papers used by Scholastic Children's Books are made from wood grown in sustainable forests.

2 4 6 8 10 9 7 5 3 1

www.scholastic.co.uk

Contents

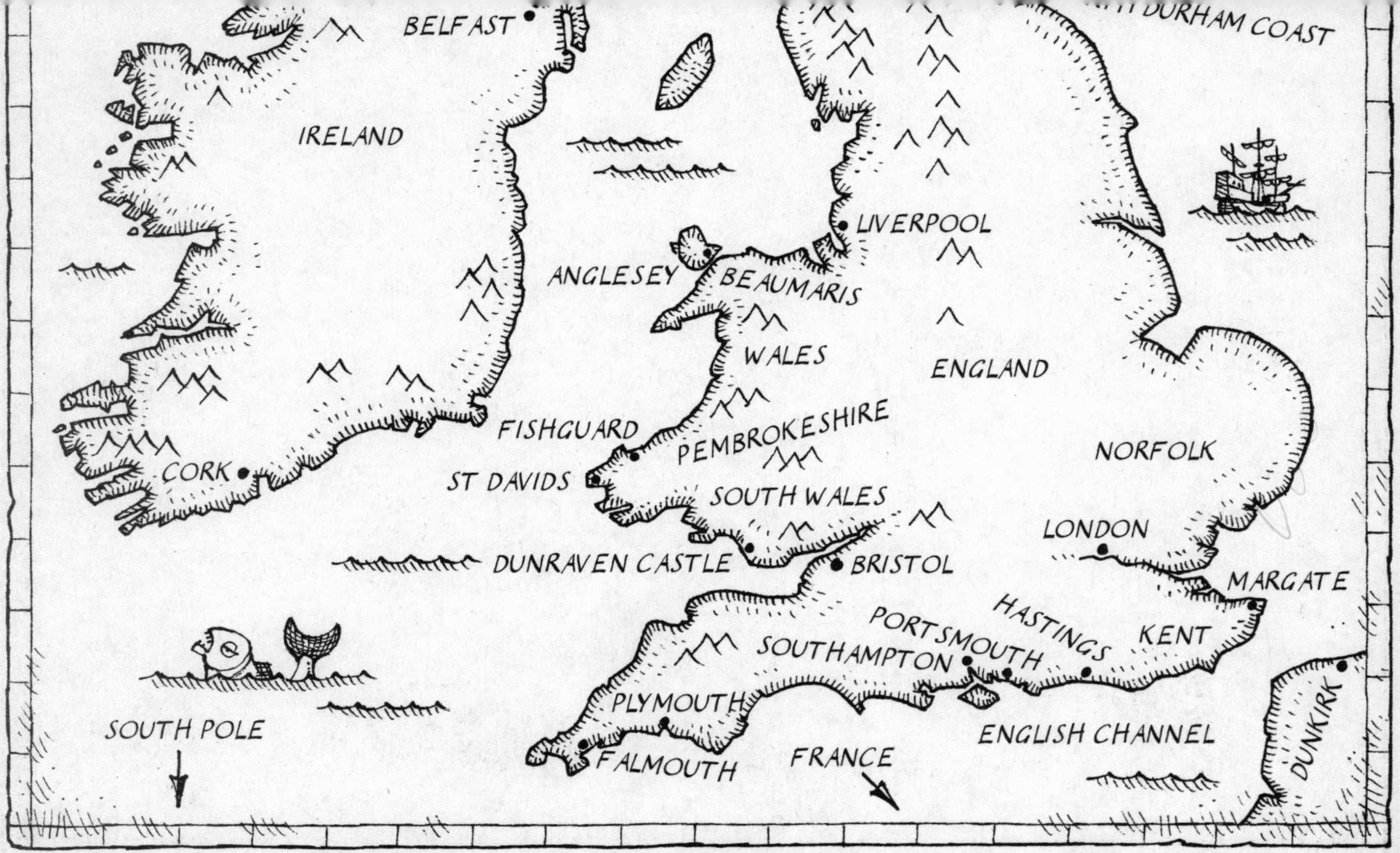

BELFAST
DURHAM COAST
IRELAND
LIVERPOOL
ANGLESEY
BEAUMARIS
WALES
ENGLAND
FISHGUARD
PEMBROKESHIRE
NORFOLK
CORK
ST DAVIDS
SOUTH WALES
LONDON
DUNRAVEN CASTLE
BRISTOL
MARGATE
HASTINGS
PORTSMOUTH
KENT
SOUTHAMPTON
PLYMOUTH
SOUTH POLE
ENGLISH CHANNEL
FALMOUTH
FRANCE
DUNKIRK

INTRODUCTION

If you live in Britain, then take your dog for a walk. If you haven't got a dog then your pet hamster, goldfish or tortoise will do.

Walk in a straight line, to the east or the west, and sooner or later you will come to the sea. Obviously it will be 'sooner' if you own a greyhound and 'later' if you take your tortoise. (A *lot* later. And if you own a pet snail don't bother. Hire a helicopter.)

In Ireland some children find wicked fairies at the bottom of their garden. They take them and tip them off high cliffs when they get to the sea. On a wintry night you can hear the ghostly song of the wet creatures...

But let's get back to your march to the sea with your dog or duck. The reason you'll come to the sea is because the British Isles are isles. (You probably guessed that from the name.)

People of the Isles have lived by the sea for thousands of years. A history book will tell you all about them. But what you really want to know is all about the people who have died by the sea. A sort of *Horrible Histories* book.

The history books will tell you of the bold song that told the British people to take over the seas in their ships. Posh Street Primary still sing it for their history teacher...

Meanwhile at Awesome Avenue Academy they sing for their *Horrible Histories* teacher.

If you're an Awesome Academy sort of student, then you need a *Horrible Histories* book that tells you all the terrible tales without getting your feet wet.

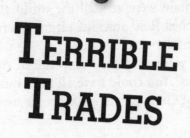

TERRIBLE TRADES

The sea brought a lot of good trade to Britain. But it also let some people invent cruel and wicked ways to make a living.

Wreckers – South Wales

Ships from Britain went around the world and came back loaded with riches. The precious cargoes were unloaded at the docks and traders came to buy.

But what if you could get a ship full of cargo before it got to the docks? You could have all the valuable stuff and not pay a penny. Great for the poor people who lived beside the sea.

Sometimes ships were blown too close to the shore and shipwrecked on rocks. But at other times men and women tricked the captains into running their ships on to rocks. These ruthless shore-robbers were known as wreckers.

Did you know...

Some of the people of Pentregethin in Wales said they had magical powers. They sold winds to the foolish villagers. They said the winds would drive ships on to the rocks and make the villagers rich. The villagers paid.

EAT THESE MAGIC BEANS AND YOU'LL GET YOUR WIND

OOOOOH!

One of the most cunning wreckers was Sir Walter Vaughan. In the days of the Slimy Stuarts, the Vaughan family owned Dunraven Castle on the shore of South Wales and were wealthy lords of Glamorgan. Walter Vaughan could be a cruel man...

As a magistrate he was a harsh judge and that eventually led to his downfall. One local thief called Matthew was sentenced to have his thieving hand chopped off.

MATTHEW HAD AN IRON HAND FITTED AND BECAME KNOWN AS MATT OF THE IRON HAND

MUST HAVE MADE IT HARD TO WIPE HIS NOSE

Soon, Walter Vaughan wasted his family fortune on rich living and found himself desperate for cash. That's when he came up with a villainous plan. He called Matt of the Iron Hand to the castle one day...

WHAT DOES LORD WALTER VAUGHAN WANT WITH A SIMPLE FARMHAND LIKE ME?

I WANT THE HELP OF YOUR VILLAINOUS FRIENDS TO DO A SPOT OF WRECKING

I'VE HEARD IT PAYS WELL

ON STORMY NIGHTS I WILL SET UP A LANTERN IN MY OLD IVY-COVERED TOWER ON THE CLIFF TOP. SHIPS IN TROUBLE WILL SEE IT AND THINK IT IS A SAFE HARBOUR LIGHT. WHEN THEY HEAD TOWARDS IT...

THEY'LL CRASH ON TO THE ROCKS AT WITCHES POINT AND MY MEN'LL TAKE THE CARGO

WE'LL STORE IT IN THE CAVES AT THE TOP OF THE CLIFF TILL I HAVE TIME TO SELL IT

IF THE SURVIVORS REPORT US WE'LL HANG

THERE MUST BE NO SURVIVORS, MATT. YOUR MEN WILL FINISH OFF ANYONE WHO SWIMS ASHORE FROM THE WRECK AND THROW THEM BACK INTO THE SEA

AFTER WE'VE ROBBED THE CORPSE

NATURALLY. WE HAVE A DEAL? LET'S SHAKE HANDS ON IT

I DON'T HAVE A HAND, MASTER VAUGHAN, AS YOU VERY WELL KNOW

So, they began their wicked trade of wrecking.

But had Matt of the Iron Hand forgiven Vaughan? Don't be daft. Of course he hadn't. Matt just waited for the right moment to get his revenge. It came one night when a fine ship was smashed on the rocks below Dunraven Castle...

A FINE PRIZE TONIGHT, MATT?

AYE, AND THE FINEST CAME FROM A MAN WHO WAS WASHED ASHORE

ALIVE?

HE WAS WHEN HE LANDED BUT I FINISHED HIM OFF MYSELF. I NOTICED HE HAD A VALUABLE RING ON HIS HAND. I COULDN'T GET THE RING OFF SO I CUT OFF THE HAND

WHERE IS IT, MATT?

I HAVE IT HERE, MASTER VAUGHAN

THE RING! I KNOW THE RING. IT ... IT IS MY RING. I GAVE IT TO MY SON... YOU MURDERED MY SON!

NO, MASTER VAUGHAN, WRECKING WAS YOUR IDEA. YOU MURDERED YOUR SON

Walter Vaughan never recovered they say. He took to drinking and wandering the beach where his son was murdered.

Did you know...

A Welsh seaman, Colyn Dolphyn, was a ruthless wrecker and kidnapper. But one of Colyn's victims lured Colyn on to rocks near St Donats and captured him. Some say he was burned alive at Llantwit Major near Cardiff and others say he was buried up to his neck on the beach. When the tide came in, it was one drowned Dolphyn.

See:
Dunraven Castle is gone and is replaced by a house built after Walter Vaughan's time. It is near Witches Point in Glamorgan.

Slave traders – Bristol, Liverpool

British sailors learned to sail the world. Some were explorers who returned with fantastic stories. Others were greedy men who went out to make a fortune ... no matter how much misery they caused. The seas made Britain rich from trade. Sometimes the trade was buying and selling people.

The first slavers

Queen Elizabeth I's sailors began buying cheap slaves in Africa, taking them across to America and swapping them for sugar, tobacco and cotton. Then they would sail back to Britain to sell the goods and make a fortune.

Slaves were worth a lot of money but the traders didn't take very good care of them. Many died, packed into dark, stinking rooms below the decks of the ships. The sailors did wash them down every day – probably a bucket of seawater thrown over the slave. (Still, that's more than slave trader Queen Elizabeth got. She only bathed four times a year. Pee-ew.)

A young slave described the journey of between forty and seventy days across the Atlantic Ocean…

The stench and the heat were dreadful. The crowding meant you hardly had room to turn over. The chains rubbed some Africans raw. The filth was made worse by the lavatory bucket and many small children fell into it. One day two of my countrymen were allowed on deck. They were chained together and decided they would rather have death than such a life of misery. They jumped into the sea.

He explained…

🌸 The 'holds' on the ship were about 1.5 metres high and slaves were allowed about half a litre of water a day.

🌸 The food was a vegetable mush and the slaves were told exactly how to eat: 'Pick up the food, put it in your mouth, swallow it.'

🌸 On long journeys, food and fresh water supplies got low. So the captain would throw weak slaves – alive – into the ocean so the fit would survive.

🌸 Slaves who died were usually thrown over the side.

Others arrived in America very sick. But the traders could deal with sick slaves – sometimes in a quite disgusting way.

One of the most common diseases was dysentery – which gives you very bad diarrhoea. Not many Americans would buy a slave with poo dribbling down their legs, would they? So what did the slave traders do?

They cut a length of rope and stuffed it up the bum of the slave with diarrhoea and blocked it for a while.

The buyers often fell for this trick.

Well, would you fancy checking?

The press gangs

'Impressment' was a word that scared many sailors. It meant the Royal Navy could come along and force you to sail on their warships. The navy bullies who grabbed you were known as a 'press gang'.

When Britain went to war in the 1730s the Navy needed

an extra 20,000 men. When the British navy fought the French in the 1790s they needed 40,000 men. The press gangs set to work.

There were armed gangs kidnapping men in their beds, or barging into weddings and dragging the groom out, much to the distress of the bride.

BUT IT'S MY BIG DAY!

Often the Royal Navy would raid a merchant ship like pirates and capture the best of the crew. But the navy was NOT allowed to press-gang foreign men. So, if they ever came for you then you'd know what to do...

WE'LL HAVE TO LEAVE HIM, BOSS

If you were a sailor or a fisherman, happy in your job, then why would you be scared of the press gangs? Because in the Royal Navy...

🌟 You would be paid less.
🌟 You may not be paid until two years had passed – to stop you deserting (running away).

ALTHOUGH, THERE'S NOT MUCH CHANCE OF ME RUNNING AWAY HERE

* If you desert then you can be hanged.
* Half the sailors on navy ships suffered when they didn't get enough fruit and vegetables. They fell ill with 'scurvy' – you begin to feel tired and weak, you have sore arms and legs, your gums begin to bleed, and you can die.
* You could be killed in a battle (or like Admiral Nelson lose an eye or an arm).

Sailors who had deserted the Royal Navy were sometimes caught in a press-gang raid. They could go back to the navy or be hanged.

The clue of the navy socks

John Hay of Scotland had run away from the navy and become a carpenter. In 1811 he was caught by a press gang and asked if he was a sailor. He tried to dodge the question.

Then one of the press gang noticed Hay had tar on his hands ... and tar was used a lot on ships. He quickly said...

He was forced to join the navy. You could have asked him...

The press gangs were not gentle. They raided the Isle of Wight on 2 April 1803 and captured two men. The people of the island tried to set the victims free. The press-gang captain fired on them, then his crew opened fire. When the shooting stopped three people had been killed. The captain was tried for murder. He was set free.

John Newton's change of heart

Some pressed men went on to have important lives. Take John Newton (1725–1807).

John was just 11 when he went to sea with his dad. When he was 17 John's dad said...

I'M GIVING UP SAILING. BUT I HAVE A GREAT JOB FOR YOU — I WANT YOU TO TAKE OVER MY SUGAR FARM IN JAMAICA AND BE A SLAVEMASTER

NO THANKS, DAD. I LIKE BEING A SAILOR SO I'M OFF TO JOIN A MERCHANT SHIP

But when he was 18 he left his ship to visit some friends. John was captured by a press gang and forced to join the Royal Navy on the ship HMS *Harwich*.

He worked well at first but then tried to desert from HMS *Harwich* and was punished in front of the crew of 350. John was stripped to the waist and flogged across his bare back.

John thought about murdering his captain. Then he thought about killing himself.

He thought HMS *Harwich* was bad. His next ship, *Pegasus*, was worse. It was a slave ship and the crew dumped him in West Africa ... to become the slave of Princess Peye. He was sure he would die there. Who would save him?

ME. HIS DAD. I PAID A SEA CAPTAIN TO RESCUE MY JOHN. NOW HE COULD DO WHAT I TOLD HIM TO YEARS AGO... BECOME A SLAVEMASTER

John began sailing the Atlantic, taking slaves from Africa to work in America. He had been a slave to Princess Peye so he knew what it was like. Would he be a kind slave trader?

I BECAME ONE OF THE WORST SLAVEMASTERS TO SAIL THE SEVEN SEAS

THAT'S MY BOY

There were sometimes slave revolts on the ships. John Newton mounted guns and muskets on the desk aimed at the slaves' quarters. Slaves were lashed and put in thumbscrews to keep them quiet.

In 1754, before he was 30, he fell ill and gave up sailing. He still put money into the slave business.

Then, three years later, he suddenly decided to become a priest. He began writing hymns and his most famous one is still sung today...

Amazing grace, how sweet the sound
That saved a wretch like me
I once was lost, but now am found
Was blind, but now I see

He began to hate the life he had led and started to argue that slavery should be stopped. He said...

It will always be a shameful memory to me, that I was once a master in a business at which my heart now shudders.

John Newton spent the rest of his life working towards the abolition of slavery.

In February 1807, the British government passed a law to abolish the slave trade.

By then John Newton, almost blind and near death, said he 'rejoiced to hear the wonderful news'.

THAT REALLY IS AMAZING GRACE

YES IT IS. BUT MY NAME'S NOT GRACE

Did you know...

In 1700, Bristol and Liverpool were small
fishing ports. As a result of the slave trade
they grew over the next 100 years and some
slave traders became enormously rich. Many of
Bristol's and Liverpool's fine buildings were
built with the profits of slavery. As a Bristol
man put it: 'Every brick in the city of Bristol
is cemented with the blood of a slave.'

See:
The International Slavery Museum, Liverpool. Find out about the lives
of slaves in Africa and in the Americas.

HEROES & VILLAINS

BOOM
BOOM
BANG

DO YOU
MIND?

BANG
BOOM
BOOM

What is a hero? A person who does something really brave. Something that most of us wouldn't even dare to do. And in our head our heroes are strong and powerful...

In real life we have heroes who help people – nurse Florence Nightingale maybe – and war heroes. In 2007 the British people voted Admiral Lord Nelson – a sailor – the greatest war hero.

Admiral Nelson (1758–1805) – Norfolk

Was young Horatio Nelson strong and powerful? No, he was a weedy and sickly child – the sixth of 11 children. Dad was no war hero either – he was a vicar – and his mum died when he was 9.

Even when Nelson grew up, he was just 163 cm tall. He didn't do a very good job growing. He had a short body and a short life to match. Here's his tragic tale...

HORATIO THE HERO NELSON
– HIS HORRIBLE LIFE –

HORATIO JOINED THE NAVY WHEN HE WAS 12. THE WEAK BOY WAS FOREVER BEING SEASICK

BLURGH

IT'S STILL BETTER THAN SCHOOL

IN 1798 BRITAIN WAS AT WAR WITH FRANCE. NELSON WON A GREAT VICTORY IN THE BATTLE OF THE NILE

I ATTACKED THE FRENCH FROM THE SIDE THEY DIDN'T EXPECT. SNEAKY SAILOR

MON DIEU!

NELSON LOST AN EYE AND AN ARM. IN BATTLES, HE CALLED HIS LOST ARM...

MY FIN

AT THE BATTLE OF COPENHAGEN, HIS LEADER SENT A SIGNAL FOR NELSON TO RETREAT. HE HELD A TELESCOPE TO HIS BLIND EYE AND SAID...

I REALLY DO NOT SEE THE SIGNAL

IN 1805 HE FOUGHT THE FRENCH AND SPANISH FLEETS AT TRAFALGAR. HE SENT A FAMOUS SIGNAL TO THE OTHER SHIPS...

ENGLAND EXPECTS THAT EVERY MAN WILL DO HIS DUTY

THE ENEMY LINED UP THEIR SHIPS. NELSON DIDN'T LINE UP OPPOSITE. HE CUT THROUGH THE LINE AND DESTROYED THEM!

THEY DIDN'T EXPECT THAT EITHER. SLY SAILOR

MON DIEU!

DIOS MIO!

NELSON PUT ON HIS FINEST UNIFORM AND GLITTERING MEDALS. CAPTAIN HARDY WARNED HIM...

THE ENEMY GUNNER WILL SEE YOU AND TARGET YOU. TAKE OFF THE MEDALS

I WON THEM IN HONOUR AND I WILL DIE IN THEM

A FRENCH MARINE SHOT NELSON AND HE FELL TO THE DECK

I AM A DEAD MAN, HARDY. I AM GOING FAST

AND SURE ENOUGH, HE WENT

Nelson was such a hero, his men knew he would have to be taken back to Britain for a great funeral. But his body would rot in the two months it took to sail all the way to London. So, they pickled it in a barrel of brandy.

There are stories that the sailors drank the brandy – probably not true.

Admiral Lord Nelson was given a statue on a 52-metre column which was placed in a London square. The square was named after his last battle – Trafalgar Square.

In the Second World War (1939–1945) the German leader, Adolf Hitler, said he would invade Britain and carry Nelson's Column back to Germany. But the British navy kept the enemy out ... again.

I'M PLEASED ABOUT THAT

Did you know...

Nelson led the Royal Navy at Trafalgar because it was his job. But 120,000 of his sailors had been forced to join the British ships. The press gangs said, 'Join the navy and you may be shot or blown up – refuse to join the navy and you'll be hanged. Which do you choose?' Which would YOU choose?

Nelson's victims

Horatio Nelson became a British hero, which is a bit odd. His mission was to go out and kill people, and he did a very good job. At the Battle of the Nile there were some sad young victims.

The captain of the French ship, *Orient*, was killed by Nelson's cannon and the ship caught fire. The captain's son had been taught never to leave his post until his commander ordered him to. But his commander – his dad – was dead.

No order? The boy stayed where he was and died when the ship's gunpowder supplies exploded under his feet. THAT was a hero for you. Such a hero, he was remembered by one of the most famous poems of Victorian times.

The boy stood on the burning deck
Whence all but he had fled;
The flame that lit the battle's wreck
Shone round him o'er the dead.

The flames rolled on – he would not go
Without his father's word;
That father, faint in death below,
His voice no longer heard.

By Felicia Hemans

It was so famous school children were told to learn it. And, children being children, they learned to make fun of it.

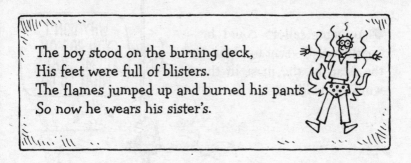

The boy stood on the burning deck,
His feet were full of blisters.
The flames jumped up and burned his pants
So now he wears his sister's.

So, a brave boy is made fun of. The man who blew him up is Britain's greatest war hero and gets a statue that everyone can see.

Nelson's heroes

Horatio Nelson was the commander of a navy at a time when sailors were treated badly. And Nelson was as cruel as any of his captains.

The punishment for doing wrong on a ship was to be flogged. And, if you worked on Nelson's ships, one man in every four would be flogged.

What did the men do?

🌸 Drank too much
🌸 Were cheeky to the officers
🌸 Were lazy.

And the punishments were...

🌸 12 to 36 lashes on the bare back
🌸 Thieves would have to walk between rows of shipmates who would beat them with knotted ropes
🌸 Sailors could be locked in leg irons on the deck, eating only bread and water

❀ Younger sailors could be 'mastheaded' – sent up to sit at the head of the mast in the wind and cold.

And the toughest punishment of all was for men who ran away from a battle – deserters. They could be 'flogged around the fleet' – rowed from ship to ship and flogged on each one. They might receive up to 300 lashes, which maybe killed them. Others were hanged and that DID kill them. No maybe.

The records for Nelson's ship, *Victory*, can still be seen...

> *Saturday 13 April 1867 at Portsmouth*
>
> *Punished M. Hollis Boy with 24 cuts with a birch for being absent 63 hours and selling part of his clothes.*

See:
National Maritime Museum, Greenwich, and learn about Horatio Nelson and his times.
HMS *Victory* - Nelson's ship at Portsmouth Historic Dockyard

What about heroes who risked their lives to SAVE people at sea? What happened to them? Heroes like Grace Darling.

Heroes: Grace Darling – Northumberland

Nelson's victory at Trafalgar meant that Britain was safe from being invaded by France. But the war went on another ten years and finally ended when France lost the Battle of Waterloo in June 1815.

Five months later a new hero was born at Bamburgh in the northeast of England.

Her name was Grace Darling. She was the seventh child in a family of nine. Her father, William, looked after the Longstone Rock lighthouse and her life was simple. Simply BORING to you or me. She helped her mother look after the lighthouse, helped her father to keep the lighthouse lamp burning, helped her brothers mend their fishing nets.

And then – in one night – her life changed. The newspapers of the time turned her from a zero to a hero...

NORTHUMBERLAND TIMES

7 September 1838

AMAZING GRACE

Last night's storm brought death and heroism to our coasts. The daughter of Longstone lighthouse keeper, William, is the amazing Grace Darling. This marvellous maid looked from the window of the lighthouse and saw a scene of horror. The paddle steamer, Steam Ship *Forfarshire*, was sailing to Dundee when her engines failed. The captain raised the sails but, in the raging northeast gale, it blew the ship on to the deadly Harcar Rocks.

Young Grace saw the front of the ship, but the back had been washed away and taken the lives of 48 people with it. A few were left on the rocks but would be washed away before the lifeboat could reach them. Grace and her father set off in their own rowing boat in spite of the gale and rescued nine people.

Grace Darling will be the darling of the British people. She must be rewarded.

William Darling and Grace received silver medals for their courage. But it was Grace's story that was remembered. Money and presents began to arrive at the lighthouse. Queen Victoria sent her £50 and letters asked for pieces of Grace's hair or just her autograph. There were some odd letters...

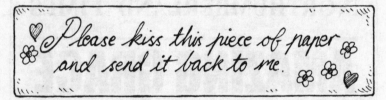

Please kiss this piece of paper and send it back to me.

Grace tried to answer all the letters and thank people for their gifts. But it can be hard to be that famous. People began to hire boats and row across to Longstone; they hoped to see Grace, meet her or touch her. A dozen painters set out to paint her picture.

The world's worst poet, William McGonagall, wrote an awful poem for her with lines like...

34

Then Grace and her father took each an oar in hand,
And to see Grace Darling rowing the picture was grand.

And as the little boat to the sufferers drew near,
Poor souls, they tried to raise a cheer;
But as they gazed upon the heroic Grace,
The big tears trickled down each sufferer's face.

And nine persons were rescued almost dead with the cold
By modest and lovely Grace Darling, that heroine bold.

Her tale was printed in Japan, Australia and America. She was invited to appear in a circus in Edinburgh. Can you picture it?

Grace almost said 'Yes' to the circus. The ladies of Edinburgh told her she'd be a fool to make an exhibition of herself. Grace wept when she saw how people were trying to use her fame.

It was all too much for the young woman. She grew weak and ill. She caught the deadly tuberculosis disease – known as 'consumption' – and moved to a house in a nearby town away from the lighthouse.

But still people pestered her. Every knock on the door was like a knock on the nail of her coffin. On the evening of Thursday 20 October 1842, Grace died in her father's arms. She was 26.

As McGonagall finished his poem...

> *Consumption, that fell destroyer, carried her away*
> *To heaven, I hope, to be an angel for ever and a day.*

Awwww. How sweet is that. Sickly sweet?

See:
Grace Darling Museum, Bamburgh, Northumberland. You can see her earwax scraper.

So now you know. If you want to be a hero like Grace Darling go out and save people. But if you want to be Britain's greatest hero, like Horatio Nelson, go out and kill hundreds of people. Simple really.

Jack Crawford

Lord Nelson was a commander of the ships. But what about the ordinary sailors who fought – and died – on those ships? Sailors like Jack Crawford.

Jack was born on 22 March 1775 in the east end of Sunderland. In 1797, when Jack was aged 22, he was serving on board HMS *Venerable*, the leading ship of Admiral Duncan's fleet. This was a very dangerous year for England.

The French, led by Napoleon, were winning all the battles on land.

The French had forced the navies of Holland and Spain to join them in the war. There were now three strong navies lined up to fight against Britain. If they joined up in the open seas they would smash the British navy and invade.

Admiral Duncan had the task of watching the Dutch fleet and stopping them from leaving their harbour. He knew ...

When the Dutch fleet came out of the harbour a terrific fight followed. A shell broke the top part of the *Venerable*'s mast and the admiral's flag fell to the deck. The admiral's flag going down was a sign to the rest of the fleet to cease fire and sail away.

Shells were flying everywhere, and the air was thick with bullets. While Jack was nailing the flag a splinter from a shot struck the mast and went through his cheek. But thanks to Jack Crawford, the flag and the British fleet were saved, the battle won.

After the battle, Jack had to be fed through a straw for six weeks, because of his wounds.

After the peace, Jack was sent on board the *America* before he returned to Sunderland. Jack Crawford was named a national hero.

The people of Sunderland were proud of their local hero and to show their love of him he was presented with a large silver medal, engraved...

THE TOWN OF SUNDERLAND
TO JACK CRAWFORD
FOR GALLANT SERVICES
ON OCT 11TH 1797

In 1831 a ship brought the deadly disease cholera to Sunderland. One of the first to die was Jack Crawford. The disease did what French shells and bullets couldn't.

See:
Mowbray Park, Sunderland: in 1890, a statue was put up in Mowbray Park, Sunderland. It shows Jack Crawford in the act of nailing the flag to the mast.
Sunderland Museum: Jack Crawford's medal is on display.

Villains – smugglers and pirates

Smugglers and pirates are remembered in children's books as jolly men and women, out for a bit of adventure.

There's a sweet English poem about smugglers, with the cute chorus:

Five and twenty ponies,
Trotting through the dark –
Brandy for the parson,
'Baccy for the clerk;
Laces for a lady, letters for a spy,
And watch the wall, my darling,
while the gentlemen go by.

The poem is supposed to be a mother talking to her little daughter. She's saying DON'T go blabbing to the soldiers about these smugglers because they're really nice chaps.

Things like brandy and 'baccy' (tobacco) came to England in ships and a tax had to be paid. But if smugglers landed the stuff secretly at night in a quiet spot then you could dodge the tax. Result? Cheap brandy and 'baccy.

The trouble is those smugglers were not 'gentlemen'… and most were not 'gentle' men. They were thugs. In 1748 William Galley, a tax collector, and David Chater, set off to go to court. They were going to tell a judge all about the Hawkhurst smuggling gang from Kent.

They stopped for a drink, where friends of the Hawkhurst gang met them. They…

* Got them drunk
* Tied their victims back-to-back
* Sat them on a horse
* Whipped them till Galley fell unconscious and then buried him alive
* Threw Chater down a 9-metre well
* Piled stones down the well to make sure he was dead.

IS THAT WHAT THEY CALL OVERKILL?

Murder for the sake of cheap booze and tobacco? Gentlemen? Would you 'turn your face to the wall'? Better not – the wall may be splashed with blood.

And if the smugglers didn't get you, the ordinary people could.

The trouble with smuggling was that a lot of poor people liked smuggling because it brought them cheap tea and cloth and brandy and tobacco. They hated the law men who tried to arrest the smugglers.

Smuggler George Ransley of Kent

Imagine you are living in the 1800s and you are poor.

WE ARE SO POOR OUR FAMILY HUDDLE ROUND A CANDLE TO KEEP WARM

AND WHEN IT TURNS REALLY COLD, WE LIGHT IT

What you need is money, and there is money to be made from smuggling. How do you START?

Why not ask George Ransley?

1. Ransley: I was a simple cart driver. But one day I found a smuggler's hoard of brandy. I sold it and made enough money to buy a house by the sea.

2. Smugglers began to use my house to land their goods. The leader was Cephas Quested. But old Cephas made a big mistake.

3. In the Battle of Brookland in 1821 Cephas sent 250 men to collect a smuggled cargo. The law men were waiting and there was a battle.

4. Cephas was too drunk to fire his musket. He handed the gun to a young man and said, 'Blow a law officer's brains out.'

5. But the young man WAS one of the law officers. He arrested Cephus who was sent for trial and hanged.

6. The Aldington Gang needed a new leader and they chose me. I did well till I was arrested and 'transported' to Australia for the rest of my life. Oh well.

George Ransley turned the gang into a business and was a popular leader. How did he do that?

🌸 The gang was run like a small army

🌸 He hired a doctor to join them in case a smuggler was wounded

🌸 A lawyer was hired to get smugglers free when they were arrested

🌸 If a smuggler was killed Ransley made sure their family was given money.

A law officer was shot in a raid – Ransley was sentenced to hang but it was at night and no one was sure who fired the shot so the judge sent Ransley to Australia instead.

Ransley had been a farmer and he did well on his farm on the other side of the world. After a couple of years his wife joined him ... along with their ten children. He died of fever at the age of 71.

So now you know how to be a rich smuggler ... organise your gang and look after the families.

Just don't get caught or you'll end up kangaroo-spotting.

THE RABBITS ARE BIG HERE, PAPA

Did you know...

The Aldington Gang were vicious, but they enjoyed a good laugh. They captured a law officer and blindfolded him. The gang told him he was to be thrown over a cliff. He managed to cling on to tufts of grass at the edge. He hung there, legs dangling and arms getting tired, fingers getting weak. At last the blindfold slipped enough that he saw his feet were just centimetres above the ground. The 'cliff' was just over two metres high. Do NOT try this on a policeman. Maybe your teacher?

See:
The Walnut Tree Inn, Aldington. There is a small window where Ransley's gang would shine a signal to their friends. George Ransley still haunts the inn.

WHAT? HE HAUNTS A PUB IN THE UK? ALL THE WAY FROM AUSTRALIA? HE DIED AND WAS BURIED IN TASMANIA!

Edinburgh violence

Smugglers brought booze into Edinburgh. It was cheap. The Scots liked that. The government didn't.

In 1736 the army started catching, arresting and executing smugglers. The people didn't like that. It led to trouble.

In Edinburgh, in March 1736, crowds gathered to watch the hanging of smuggler Andrew Wilson.

Wilson was taken from his cell in chains at 2 p.m. A report said...

> All was hush, Psalms sung, prayers said for an hour or more and the man hanged with all decency and quietness.

A large crowd had gathered at the Grassmarket and so Captain of the Guard, John Porteous, ordered his soldiers to guard the prisoner. The executioner managed to hang Wilson. But trouble began soon after...

> Some unlucky boys threw a stone or two at the hangman, which is very common. Porteous ordered his party to load their guns and fire over the heads of the mob. But they left three men, a boy and a woman dead upon the spot.

The people of Edinburgh were shocked. They said that Porteous should be arrested for murder. He was. That same afternoon.

Porteous was found guilty and sentenced to death. The Edinburgh folk were happy with that and looked forward to the execution. Porteous was locked in the Old Tolbooth.

But the mob couldn't wait. The gates were smashed and a gang of men rushed for the prison cells. Captain Porteous was dressed in his nightshirt.

The mob dragged him through the streets, and no one tried to stop them. They took him to the Grassmarket where Andrew Wilson had been hanged. They had no time to build new gallows, so they threw the rope from a draper's shop over a dyer's pole outside another shop.

The rioters hauled Porteous up and he met his end. No one was punished for his murder, and the smuggling went on.

> **See:**
> The Old Tolbooth is gone but Canongate Tolbooth on the Royal Mile, South Queensferry Tolbooth and the tolbooth in Dean Village can still be seen.

Edward 'Blackbeard' Teach

Maybe you've heard the song, sung by sailors. Sailing songs are called 'shanties' and this one is weird and a little bit creepy...

> *Fifteen men on the Dead Man's Chest*
> *Yo-ho-ho, and a bottle of rum*
> *Drink and the devil had done for the rest*
> *Yo-ho-ho, and a bottle of rum*

From *Treasure Island* by Robert Louis Stevenson
But what is 'the Dead Man's Chest'?
a) an island
b) a ship
c) a corpse

Answer: the 'Dead Man's Chest' was one of the British Virgin Islands in the Atlantic.

The Dead Man's Chest

Forget the fun stories of pirates sailing around pinching gold and burying it on treasure islands. Real pirates were men and women who sailed around looking for harmless trading ships to attack. They were nasty bullies.

The true story of the Dead Man's Chest shows just how nasty they could be.

In the early 1700s the pirate Edward Teach – known as 'Blackbeard' – decided to punish his crew because they didn't do as they were told.

SO, TEACH WAS LIKE MY TEACHER... HE GIVES ME DETENTION AND IF I DON'T DO WHAT I'M TOLD, I GET LOCKED AWAY ALONE

Blackbeard's detention was a bit tougher than a school detention. He sailed to the island of Dead Man's Chest, put them on the island then sailed away.

The island was just 250 square metres, it had no water and had cliffs all around. There was nowhere for them to launch a boat and sail to safety. Leaving someone on an island is called 'marooning'.

Blackbeard gave each man a pirate sword – a cutlass - and a bottle of rum. He thought the rum would make them drunk and then they would kill each other.

But when he returned at the end of 30 days, he found that 15 had survived. There was only rainwater to drink but for food there were pelicans, lizards and snakes to eat.

Teach was worse than any teacher. But he'd be a great teacher of pirates...

PASS THE PELICAN PÂTÉ, PLEASE

HOW TO BE A PIRATE...

by Edward 'Blackbeard' Teach

1. Start young. I was born in Bristol and went to sea when I was a boy. I fought for the British navy. I became a good sailor and expert shot. I also learned how the British ran their ships and their crews – later I would use that against them.

Lesson: Inside knowledge is useful.

2. Learn from the best. I met Captain Benjamin Hornigold in 1716 – a fearsome pirate in the West Indies. I joined his crew. I was ace at hand-to-hand combat, and soon commanded a small ship for Hornigold.

Lesson: Listen to your teacher.

3. Look fearsome. I was tall and strong but made myself more fearsome by growing this beard which grew up to my eyes. I would twist and braid it into black ribbons and then tuck them behind my ears.

Lesson: It pays to look scary.

4. Arm yourself. I wore a belt across my chest that held several matchlock pistols. The burning fuses I used to light the pistols were tucked beneath my hat. They made large clouds of stinking smoke which made it seem as if I was afire.

Lesson: Always have a bucket of water handy in case of accidents.

5. Arm yourself some more. Round my waist I wore a wide leather belt with swords, axes, daggers and more pistols. I often called for the Devil to help me as I swore terrible oaths and curses. And I gave myself a good name.

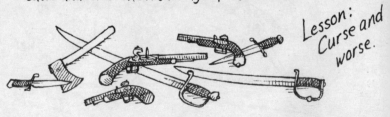

Lesson: Curse and worse.

6. **Arm your ship.** My ship was named Queen Anne's Revenge and fitted with 40 guns. When I was close to a merchant ship I ran up the red flag to show I was a pirate. The black flag meant 'surrender or die'.

Lesson: Don't let your victim know you're going to rob them till it's too late.

7. **Scare your enemy, don't hurt them.** (Unless they resist.) I never beat or killed any captives who gave up quietly. I treated women passengers with respect and care. But I was ruthless and murderous to the ones who tried to fight back.

Lesson: Keep your promises and your threats.

8. **Be ready to die fighting.** I met a British navy ship and was defeated. I fought the navy captain but I was cut in the neck from behind. The rumour was that my head was lopped off and my body was thrown in the sea and swam three times round the ship before it sank.

Lesson: Get used to the idea you'll be caught and killed.

APART FROM THE BLACK BEARD, I COULD BE A PIRATE. BETTER THAN SCHOOL

Just before you set off to join a pirate ship, look at the story of William Kidd...

Captain Kidd (1645–1701) – Tilbury, London

So, pirate matey, those are wise words: 'Get used to the idea you'll be caught and killed.' Captain William Kidd did NOT expect to be killed.

Kidd THOUGHT he'd done a good job for Britain. He was sure he'd be treated like a hero. He ended up a hanged hero.

✱ Kidd was born in Dundee, Scotland. Some people believe his dad was a priest. He sailed to New York and worked on Captain Jean Fantin's ship. Fantin took treasure from a Spanish ship but the crew thought he didn't give them a fair share. One night, when Fantin went ashore, Kidd led a gang

THE *BLOOD-SOAKED WILLIAM* MORE LIKE

who killed the guards and stole the ship. The ship was given a new name, the *Blessed William* ... William Kidd, get it?

✱ Britain went to war with France. The British king gave Kidd the job of attacking enemy ships. Kidd would not be paid, but he could take the enemy ships and all their cargoes. He wasn't part of the Royal Navy. He was part of a private navy, so these captains got the name 'privateers'. Kidd set off for the Indian Ocean in 1696.

🌸 It was a bit of a disaster. A third of his crew died of cholera and his ship began to leak. A crew man called William Moore argued with Kidd and Captain Kidd picked up an iron bucket and smashed it over the man's head. Moore died.

🌸 Kidd wasn't very good at finding pirates, but after two years he came across a ship with £70,000 worth of silks and sugar. Instead of capturing pirates he became one and took the ship and its cargo. Then he found the captain was English and wanted to set the ship free. Kidd's crew refused so he went ahead with the pirate act.

🌸 He left Britain in 1696 as a privateer. But, while he was away, the law changed and by the time he was caught in 1698 a privateer had become a pirate. Not only that, but he was charged with the murder of William Moore. He was sentenced to be hanged.

🌸 Captain William Kidd was hanged on 23 May 1701. The first rope put around his neck broke, so he had to be strung up a second time. His corpse was placed in an iron cage gibbet at the mouth of the River Thames. It was left there to rot. Sailors passed it on their way up the river to London. It was a warning: 'This is what happens to pirates.'

Still want to be a pirate?

Did you know...

Ships that sailed down the River Thames had to salute the Queen's yacht when they saw it. In 1696 Kidd's crew didn't bother to do that. The Queen's ship fired a cannon at them to teach them a lesson. Kidd's crew 'saluted' by dropping their trousers and slapping their bottoms at the Queen's ship. Kidd's rude crew were arrested and forced to sail with the Royal Navy.

I THINK IT'S A TWENTY-ONE BUM SALUTE

See:
No one knows the actual site of Execution Dock – the gallows are long gone. But a copy is still in place by the Prospect of Whitby pub. Go down Wapping High Street from the Overground station and look out for the Town of Ramsgate pub. Look out for a small passageway that leads to Wapping Old Stairs. Go down the stairs and you'll be on the riverbanks near where Captain Kidd died.

DISASTERS & TRIUMPHS

ICE WITH YOUR MARTINI, SIR?

Take some planks of wood. Fasten them together to make a ship. Put up a mast and lift up a sail. Then launch it into the sea.

Safe as sitting in bed, you would think. If it sinks you just swim ashore. But sail a bit further and you can't even see the shore. If the wind drives the waves higher than your mast then your planks begin to creak and split.

Safe as sitting in bed while your house is on fire. You find you are in the middle of...

...A DISASTER

The *White Ship* – English Channel

In the last Ice Age, Britain and Ireland were joined to Europe. You could walk across to France. The ice melted, the waters rose and washed away the land between Britain and France. It made a channel we call the English Channel.

Many people have discovered just how deadly the English Channel can be.

The Normans managed to cross the Channel when they invaded England in 1066. They landed at Hastings, marched up to London and crowned William as their king.

Those old Normans believed men should rule, so when William I died his sons took the throne. First came William II ... but he died, shot with an arrow while he was out hunting. Maybe his brother, Henry, had something to do with it?

When Henry died, his son, William Adelin, was meant to get the throne ... but the English Channel got him first.

One man lived to tell the tale of the disaster – Berold, a butcher from Rouen. If Berold had written a letter to Henry I it may have looked like this...

25 November 1120

Your Royal Highness,

I write from my butcher shop with a bit of bad news. When I say a BIT of bad news, I mean a LOT of bad news. Your son, William Adelin, drowned when his ship sank.

Never mind, I lived to tell the tale, so that's all right. And your Will died a hero, I can tell you. As you know the ship set sail from Normandy to cross the English Channel. We were following your ship.

Your dear son Will was so kind he gave the crew of the *White Ship* lots of barrels of wine. They drank the lot before they set off. A bit of a mistake because you should never drink and drive a horse never mind a ship. A lot of sailors were left behind, too drunk. They were the lucky ones.

The others told the captain to have a race – catch your ship and overtake you for a lark. But it was dark. A sort of dark lark. We hit a rock and began to sink. There was just one little boat and three hundred people in the sea. Of course your son Will got into the boat and headed back to shore. I squeezed in the back.

 Then brave young Will heard cries of, 'Help me, I am Matilda, help me.' Will knew it was his half-sister so he ordered the little boat to turn back and rescue her. But there were three hundred other people trying to fight their way on to our boat. They swamped it and we all sank. Poor, brave Will drowned.

Me? I am happy to say I clung to a rock till daylight and was rescued. So that was nice, wasn't it? I know you have other kids, Your Highness, so you haven't lost everything, have you? I'm sure Will and Matilda will have lovely funerals (if their bodies are ever found). If you have a funeral feast maybe my humble butcher shop can supply the meat? I have a nice fat ox. Like your Will it is freshly slaughtered.

All the best.
Sorry for your loss, of course.

Berold the Butcher

They say that King Henry never smiled again after the disaster. He had a daughter, known as Maud, and he wanted to make her queen when he died.

A lot of barons said...

WE DON'T WANT A WOMAN ON THE THRONE OF ENGLAND. WE WANT HENRY'S NEPHEW, STEPHEN ... EVEN IF HE IS A BIT OF A WIMP

OH, THANKS, MATE

When Henry died Stephen's barons went to war with Maud's barons. The English fought the English for long and cruel, miserable years.

A monk wrote about the bitter war.

In the days of King Stephen there was nothing but fighting, evil, and robbery. The great men who were traitors rose against Stephen. When the traitors saw that Stephen was a friendly, kindly and relaxed man who inflicted no punishment, then they committed all manner of horrible crimes. And so it lasted for 19 years while Stephen was king, till the land was all undone and darkened with such deeds. Men said openly that Christ and his angels slept.

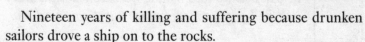

Nineteen years of killing and suffering because drunken sailors drove a ship on to the rocks.

I'M SMASHED ON THE ROCKS

VERY FUNNY

Rothsay Castle - Liverpool, Lancashire

The *Rothsay Castle* was one of the first steam-driven ships. She was built to sail up and down the River Clyde near Glasgow. She was never meant to go into the rough Irish Sea. The engine was 15 years old and not powerful enough.

If the captain's logbook had survived it may have told the tragic story ... a story of greed, stupidity and brandy.

CAPTAIN'S LOG:	Wednesday, 17 August 1831
SHIP:	Rothsay Castle
CLASS:	Paddle steamer. 200 tons. 50 horsepower.
HISTORY:	Built Glasgow 1816
OWNERS:	Liverpool and North Wales Steamship Company
CREW:	Captain Atkinson, mate, steward, two firemen, two seamen and a three-piece band. 130 passengers.
VOYAGE:	Liverpool to Beaumaris. 50 miles.
DEPARTURE:	10 a.m. 12 noon. Passenger Mr Forster from London is late arriving. Important man, so we wait. It takes more time to get his carriage on board. 2 hours late means we miss the tide and will be sailing in darkness. But I can find my

way blindfolded. We are short of three crew. They left the ship because, they said, it is too dangerous. Nonsense. They are just cowards.

4 p.m. Northwest winds gale force. We shall be very late. Passengers distressed. One asked me to turn back. He doesn't know what he is talking about. He tried to argue I am drunk. I have had a bottle of brandy but am sober as a nun. We go on.

7 p.m. Reached Little Orme headland.

10 p.m. Reached Great Orme headland. 3 hours to do the last 5 miles. Tide against us now. Engine running slow. 2 feet of water in the stokehold. Pumps not working. No buckets on board to bail out.

10:30 p.m. Crew prepared lifeboat. They report it has a hole in it and there are no paddles anyway. We won't need it.

11 p.m. Passenger Mr William Tarrey, land agent to the Earl of Derby, is asking me to turn into

Llandudno but I think we can reach Beaumaris. I told him, 'If we turn back, it will never do: there will be no profit.'

Midnight. Engine losing most of its power. We are driven by wind and tides now. Passengers helping to raise the sail instead.

1 a.m. North west winds have driven us to run aground on Dutchman Bank. I have told the panicking passengers, 'It is only sand, she will soon float.'

1:30 a.m. Report by Able Seaman James. Captain and mate swept overboard along with a hundred passengers. Ship breaking up but we will cling to what is left till daylight and rescue comes. Funnel has fallen. Lifeboat launched but swept away.

4 a.m. At last the lookout at Penmon Point has noticed the wreck. The rescue boat has been sighted. I have counted 23 of us left alive. It has been a disaster.

It was a slow death for the families. Most of the passengers were seasick; children were crying. Their mothers were fearful. Women screamed and clutched their children. A priest began to pray.

There were no flares aboard, no guns, no way of signalling for help, except for the ship's bell. Someone began to ring it, but the sound was carried away by the wind. The ship was only two miles from dry land – and ten other ships were not far away, waiting for the storm to die down.

Did you know...

John Nuttall from Bury was one of very few to have a lucky escape. He was standing on deck holding the hand of Selina Lamb. A large wave washed them overboard and the girl in her heavy skirts vanished. Nuttall couldn't swim but he managed to scramble back on to the wreck.

He saw a half-drowned woman alongside it and dragged her out of the sea by her hair. He was amazed to find it was the woman who lived next door to him, Mary Whittaker. Soon the deck under them broke free and floated away. Nuttall and another man grabbed pieces of wreckage and used them to paddle for shore.

Mary Whittaker tore off her petticoat and

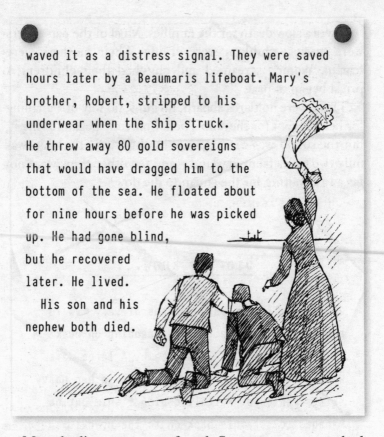

waved it as a distress signal. They were saved hours later by a Beaumaris lifeboat. Mary's brother, Robert, stripped to his underwear when the ship struck. He threw away 80 gold sovereigns that would have dragged him to the bottom of the sea. He floated about for nine hours before he was picked up. He had gone blind, but he recovered later. He lived.

His son and his nephew both died.

Many bodies were never found. Some were even washed up 100 miles away.

The angry people of Liverpool said that the *Rothsay Castle* was a leaky old tub that should never have been put to sea. The drunken captain was blamed.

The captain of the *White Ship* didn't learn from his mistake of drink-driving a ship. He was just too dead. But you would think OTHER sailors would learn the dangers of boozy boating. Yet the captain of *Rothsay Castle* was still doing it 700 years later.

At least a little good came from the *Rothsay Castle* disaster. New laws started to be made that said ships should have life jackets, lifeboats, signals and, eventually, radios, which would all make sailing safer.

See:
Puffin Island, Anglesey, Wales, is the nearest spot to where *Rothsay Castle* sank and where some survivors would have landed.

But some *Rothsay Castle* lessons were forgotten...

Titanic – Belfast, Northern Ireland

The sinking of the *Titanic* in 1912 – 80 years after the *Rothsay Castle* disaster – is probably the most famous sea disaster of all time. The great ship was built in Belfast and was said to be unsinkable. It met an iceberg and sank on its first voyage.

The *Rothsay Castle* had one crumbling lifeboat. The new laws made sure *Titanic* had a lot of lifeboats ... it just didn't have enough for over 2,200 passengers. What was the point of that? Captain Edward Smith might have explained.

Like the *White Ship* and *Rothsay Castle*, the captain of the *Titanic* died when it sank and was given the blame.

Captain Edward J Smith was accused of going too fast even though he had warnings of icebergs. However, there was one great difference between the sinking of the *Titanic* and that of the *Rothsay Castle*: the behaviour of the passengers and crew. Many people on the *Titanic* were true heroes and kept calm in the face of the danger...

Did you know...

76% of the 439 women on board survived because the rule was: 'women and children first'. Most of the men stuck to that rule. 50% of the 105 children survived but only 19% of the 1,662 men lived.

Even more women and children would have been saved but some refused to leave their husbands or fathers and chose to die with them.

There were 84 men in the boiler section of the crew. They were safely on deck but went below a dangerous second time to keep the boilers going. Only eight were saved.

There were 36 engineers in the crew – they kept the engines running until three minutes before the ship sank so there would be light for the rescuers. Not one of the engineers survived.

There were five postal clerks. They worked steadily to save the mail though the postal room was flooded at an early stage. Not one of the postal clerks survived.

There were an unknown number of ship's boys. They helped load the boats and make sure passengers had biscuits for their comfort in the lifeboats. Not one of the ship's boys survived.

Captain Edward J Smith was reported to have died on his ship crying out, 'Be British'. Other reports speak of him swimming in the sea trying to save the life of a child. He did not survive.

Of all the disasters in the history of the world the sinking of the *Titanic* has left us with one of the greatest images. A simple picture of human courage in the face of death. The last minutes of the ship's band.

The heroes

There were eight players in the band. They played dance music to relax the passengers as those passengers climbed into the boats. As the water flowed around their feet, the band played a final hymn. Then there was silence.

Their leader was Wallace Hartley, and as passengers panicked, he ordered the musicians to keep playing in an effort to keep everyone calm. As the ship kept sliding down, the band moved to the forward half of the boat deck and continued playing even when they knew they were doomed.

No one quite agreed on the last song they played. Mrs Vera Dick lived to tell the tale. She said that the final song played by the band was the hymn 'Nearer, My God, to Thee'.

Some people say Mrs Dick had left in a lifeboat more than an hour before the ship finally sank. She couldn't have known.

Harold Bride, one of the wireless operators, reported that he had heard 'A Song of Autumn'.

None of the eight musicians survived. But their courage will never be forgotten.

Nearer, my God, to thee,
Nearer to thee
Though like the wanderer,
The sun gone down,
Darkness be over me,
My rest a stone....

The legend of the cursed ship

There were about 2,224 passengers and crew aboard and more than 1,500 died. After the disaster, people said *Titanic* was always an 'unlucky' ship. She was 'cursed'.

When she left harbour on her first voyage her huge size 'sucked' two smaller ships towards her. They almost collided. If they had crashed into the *Titanic* the liner would have had to stop its voyage for repairs. She would never have then struck that iceberg. In escaping a small accident, the *Titanic* went on to a much greater disaster.

But what were these curses?

Curse 1: the Pope's revenge

Titanic was built in Belfast by the Harland and Wolff shipyard. Ireland was divided by religion. The Catholics followed the Pope while the Protestants had the British King as the head of their church.

Belfast was mainly a Protestant city and the workers at the shipyard were mainly Protestant. After the disaster, the Catholics claimed the Protestants stamped 'To hell with the Pope' on every piece of steel.

That's why the Pope prayed to his leader, God, and God cursed it and sent an iceberg to sink it.

Curse 2: Egypt's revenge

Egypt is full of tales of mummy curses. One tale says a mummified priestess was sold to America. It was loaded on to a ship and kept just behind the control room – the bridge. It is said that the mummy's curse affected the captain's judgement. It made him steer the ship into an iceberg and sink. The ship was the *Titanic*.

Some people say it can't be true.

THERE IS NOTHING WRITTEN DOWN TO SHOW THAT THERE WAS AN EGYPTIAN COFFIN ON BOARD THE *TITANIC*

AH, NO, THAT'S BECAUSE THE CAPTAIN DIDN'T RECORD THE MUMMY CARGO. HE DIDN'T WANT TO FRIGHTEN SOME OF THE PASSENGERS

Of course ALL of the passengers were frightened when the *Titanic* began to sink.

The survivor

Many of the passengers and crew died bravely. But not everyone on the *Titanic* was so brave.

J Bruce Ismay was head of the company that owned the *Titanic*. He decided to sail on that first and last voyage. It is said that he told Captain Smith to go as fast as possible to show the world how amazing the new ship was. Captain Smith told Ismay about the icebergs. Ismay told him to ignore the danger because he wanted to break the speed record.

Ismay found out he was wrong. When the ship began to

sink he jumped into one of the last lifeboats to leave and he survived. There was room in the lifeboat and he wasn't taking another person's place. But he hadn't the courage to look up and see the ship go down. A newspaper said...

> **H**e passes through the most terrible tragedy untouched and unmoved. He leaves his ship to sink with its powerless cargo of lives and does not care to lift his eyes. He crawls through awful disgrace to his own safety.

And Ismay was the man who left the ship short of lifeboats. It should have had 48. He made sure it carried just 20. He said ..

WHY LITTER THE DECK WITH USELESS BOATS WHEN THE SHIP IS HERSELF A LIFEBOAT?

Ismay became one of the most hated men in the world ... for saving his own life.

See:
The Titanic Experience, Belfast. Displays bring the *Titanic* story to life.

Sirius v. Brunel's *Great Western* – Glasgow

In the early 1800s British inventors were starting to fit steam engines into ships. The engine drove paddles and moved the ships.

Now the captains didn't have to worry about the winds dropping and leaving them stuck in the middle of the ocean. Steamships were 'the future'.

Isambard Kingdom Brunel was a proud man and a famous inventor. He wanted to show the world how great he was. And he wanted to be remembered for his greatest feat.

Brunel wanted to build the first steamship ever to cross the Atlantic Ocean, from the British Isles to the USA. He built the mighty SS *Great Western* to win the race. It was the largest ship in the world and, on 31 March 1838, sailed down the River Avon with 57 passengers.

At the same time a much smaller ship, SS *Sirius*, set sail from Cork (southern Ireland) on 4 April 1838, overloaded with coal and 45 passengers. Brunel wasn't worried. He told people...

So, SS *Sirius* had no chance. As Brunel's mighty ship set off there was a small fire in the engine room. It wasn't a big disaster, but Brunel rushed down the ship's stairway to help put the fire out. He slipped and fell 6 metres down a burning ladder. He had to be carried ashore ... and 50 passengers were so scared they decided to leave the ship too.

The *Sirius* had four days' head start. Battered Brunel still said...

SS *Sirius* was slow and not big enough to deal with the Atlantic Ocean waves, but the crew battled on. *Great Western* glided after her and every day closed the gap. When SS *Sirius* was in sight of New York the crew started burning barrels of tar to save their last bit of coal. And *Great Western* was just hours behind.

But *Sirius* won the race to be 'the first'. Brunel was a b-a-d loser.

Brunel said SS *Sirius* was too small to carry the coal it needed to cross the Atlantic. Brunel was WRONG. His friends told the newspapers an amazing story...

The story of the *Sirius* crew burning chairs to keep the ship going is a fantastic adventure tale. Everyone believed it and the story is STILL told in history books today.

But this is a *Horrible Histories* book and HH always tells the truth. The truth is SS *Sirius* DID have enough coal. When it landed in New York there were still 15 tons left.

Vanished ships

SS *Sirius* made just one more Atlantic journey before she settled on the Ireland to Scotland trips. Then disaster struck. On 16 January 1847 on a voyage to Cork from Glasgow, she struck rocks in dense fog in Ballycotton Bay, Ireland. The ship was re-floated, but was leaking badly and was wrecked on Smith's Rocks, half a mile later. Only one lifeboat could be launched and was heavily overcrowded. In the rough seas 12 passengers and two crew were drowned. Most of the 91 on board were rescued by rope line to the shore.

SS *Great Western* had a great career, crossing the Atlantic another 45 times. In 1856 she was finally broken up and scrapped in London. A sad end.

See:

Brunel's next great ship, SS *Great Britain*, can be seen at the dry dock in the Great Western Dockyard, Bristol. You can climb the mast of the huge ship – if you aren't afraid.

WARS & INVASIONS

ARE WE NEARLY THERE YET?

If you live on an island then it is hard for enemies to attack you. But it's not impossible. Some will try. Most invasions of Britain have failed.

Viking attack – Bishop Morgeneu – St Davids, Pembrokeshire

Every country has been invaded at some time. Enemies march in. Castles have moats to keep enemies out. The seas around the country SHOULD have kept invaders out of Britain. But good sailors could cross the seas to bash the Brits.

The Romans did it under Julius Caesar in 55 BC. Then came the Saxons from the north of Germany, smashing their way to power in AD 400s.

The old Britons were driven into Wales and the Saxons settled in England. But nothing is ever 'settled' in those islands.

In 793 the Vikings came over the North Sea from Denmark and Norway to attack a monastery on the northeast coast. Then they sailed round the north of the British Isles to take over Dublin in Ireland. From there they started to cross the Irish Sea to attack Wales.

The Welsh called the Vikings 'black' for some reason...

The Vikings robbed the monasteries and stole the crops from the peasants till they starved. They say the Welsh prayed for bad weather because it kept the Vikings away for a while.

At last the Welsh found a hero to defend them. Rhodri the Great, who became ruler of most of Wales by the 850s and united Wales against the invaders.

One of the most terrible tales of their attack was on St Davids Cathedral at Menevia, in the year 999. Not only did they destroy the church, they also gave Bishop Morgeneu a pretty hard time...

LET US PRAY. OH LORD, SEND BAD WEATHER. SEND FOG AND RAIN, STORMS AND LIGHTNING

HAILSTONES WOULD BE GOOD

YEAH

HAILSTONES AND TORNADOES

HUGE SEA MONSTERS IN THE IRISH SEA

SEA MONSTERS IN THE... LET'S NOT GET CARRIED AWAY. JUST A STRONG EASTERLY WIND MIGHT DO IT, GOD. THANKING YOU IN THE HOPE YOU ANSWER OUR PRAYERS. AMEN

AMEN

JUST A LITTLE SEA MONSTER?

SUDDENLY THERE WAS A KNOCK ON THE CHURCH DOOR

COME IN. WHAT IS IT, OLD WOMAN?

THERE'S A VIKING WARSHIP ON THE SHORE. THEY'LL BE HERE ANY MINUTE

GASP

MY FRIENDS. THE BLACK NATION ARE AT OUR DOORS AGAIN. IF WE GIVE THEM THE LITTLE GOLD AND JEWELS WE HAVE, THEY SHOULD GO AWAY

LET'S TRY LOCKING THE DOOR AND KEEPING QUIET. IT MIGHT WORK

77

The Vicious Vikings tied Bishop Morgeneu to a church pillar. They ripped off his fine robes. A Viking took a sharp knife and ran it all the way up his backbone to separate it from his ribs.

The Viking reached inside the ribs and pulled out the bishop's lungs. Then he spread them across his back – like the wings of an eagle. That's why they called it the blood eagle.

But the Vikings never did conquer Wales the way they did the north and east of England.

The Welsh kings like Rhodri Mawr were just too tough for them. He beat the Vikings in 856. Their leader was called Horn...

And when he died all the Viking enemies were delighted – especially the Irish.

Then there was the Sunday Battle of Anglesey in 876.

The Vikings lost that one too. The Welsh reckoned it served them right for going to war on the Sabbath.

The Vikings conquered the seas round Britain, but the Welsh kings conquered the Vikings.

See:
St Davids Bishop's Palace. The palace of the medieval bishops of St Davids is a stone's throw from St Davids Cathedral.

William the Conqueror - Hastings, Sussex

The Vikings moved south and grabbed land in the north of France where they were known as the 'North Men'… or 'Norman' for short. The Normans were great castle builders – they needed to be because nobody liked them much.

In 1066 their leader, William the Conqueror, landed on the south coast of England and defeated the English king, Harold, at the Battle of Hastings.

Terrible Tale

When the Normans landed near Hastings they found the Saxons waiting for them at the top of Senlac Hill. The knights weren't very keen on charging up the hill … the Saxons were big blokes with swords and battleaxes and the poor Normans could get hurt.

IF THE SWORDS AND AXES DON'T KILL ME, RUNNING UP THAT BLINKIN' HILL WILL

There is a legend (may even be true) that a juggler called Taillefer told them there was nothing to worry about. He rode in front of the English army and sang a song about a French hero … and juggled his sword at the same time. Clever chap.

That annoyed an English knight who rode out to attack him. Taillefer killed him. He then led William the Conqueror's troops into the Battle of Hastings. The Norman historian, Wace, said…

> *A minstrel named Taillefer went in front of the Norman army, singing and juggling with his sword while the troops marched behind singing the Song of Roland.*

Brave chap. He was swallowed up by the English army and hacked to pieces. Dead brave.

Did you know...

Hastings was the first castle the Normans built on English soil. But it was made in France. The Normans carried the pieces across the English Channel and put the bits together when they landed.

William the Conqueror became king and dished out England to his knights. They spread out and started ruling their lands. The great age of castle-building had begun. The first ones were made of wood but in time they were replaced with stone.

See:

1066 Battle Of Hastings, Abbey And Battlefield. Visit the museum and look out over the battlefield. See where King Harold is buried (maybe).

The Spanish Armada – Plymouth

One of the greatest invasions came in the days of the Terrible Tudors.

In 1587 Queen Elizabeth had her cousin, Mary Queen of Scots, locked in prison. That year Elizabeth's spies discovered a plot – Mary's friends were going to kill Elizabeth and put Mary on the throne of England. Elizabeth had Mary's head chopped off and that was the end of the plot.

PLOTS GO PLOP WITH LOPPED-OFF TOPS

But Mary had friends in Spain. King Philip II of Spain built a mighty fleet of ships – an armada. In 1588 it set sail for England. Mighty galleons should have crushed the small English ships.

BIG, AREN'T THEY?

But the sea came to England's rescue. Storms in the English Channel drove the Armada onto the beaches of Holland and the English ships attacked the helpless Spanish.

The English heroes got a medal that told the story in a few words...

GOD BLEW WITH HIS WINDS, AND THEY WERE SCATTERED

The victorious English sailors were heroes. Did Elizabeth reward them well for saving her?

Nope. The sailors were no longer needed so they were sent home. They had no jobs to go to so they soon ran out of money.

WINDY, ISN'T IT?

The sailors were left to starve, forgotten in the streets.

Disease spread through the remaining ships. The man in charge of the English ships was Lord Howard.

He wrote to Queen Elizabeth...

Your Majesty,

Our sailors have not been paid and have been left to die in ports like Plymouth. The ones who stayed on the ships have been attacked by a terrible fever. I found fresh, strong sailors to replace the dead crews, but the new men are dying faster than the old ones.

They have been at sea for eight months with no change of clothes and no money to buy fresh ones. The men who leave the ships are dying in the streets. It would break anyone's heart to see these men – who fought so bravely – die so miserably. I beg you to send money to pay their wages.

Your humble servant

Lord Howard

The Queen's paymaster, Lord Burghley, was pleased when he saw this letter. He wrote back to say...

The dead sailors need no pay. And the sick can be sent home. They will not have to be paid. A lot of money will be saved that way.

Oddly the sick sailors didn't blame the queen – they were sure bad beer was to blame for their illness.

A year later things were little better. When the ship *Dreadnought* arrived back in Plymouth from a trip to Portugal there were just 18 men fit enough to sail her – they had set off with 300.

The queen did one thing to help. She said her sailors could have a licence to beg – for a short time.

William Browne lost an arm in the Armada fighting. His licence said...

William Browne may beg in all churches for one year. By order of Her Majesty Queen Elizabeth

Some Armada ships had left behind treasure. The sailors got none of it – the queen got a large share.

A year later Elizabeth became more fierce when she ordered...

The arrest and punishment of soldiers, sailors and other jobless persons and strong beggars.

She wanted to stop them from even begging. The poor sick sailors had been described as:

These ragged rabblements of rakehells that, under the pretence of great misery, do win great alms.

85

Finally, five years after the Armada had been defeated, people like Robert Mackey received money to help them live. Mackey had lost his hands in a battle and received one payment of 33 shillings and 4 pence. That would just be enough to last him two months ... a month for each hand.

And Elizabeth? A report said she was upset at the sight of beggars when she rode out in her carriage...

The Queen is troubled, whenever she takes the air, with these miserable creatures.

Shame. Elizabeth said her treasure chests were empty. She had to struggle on with 3,000 gowns and 628 pieces of jewellery.

I COULD STRUGGLE ON WITH 628 PIECES OF JEWELLERY

That's how Britain treated its heroes of the sea. Would you want to be an English sailor in the days of the Armada?

I COULDN'T DO THAT

See:
Grange and Armada Association in at the Old Court House in Grange Village, Sligo. Learn about the events of 1588, walk the De Cuéllar Trail and see the wreck site at Streedagh Strand.

Jemima Nicholas – West Wales

Everybody remembers the first French invasion of Britain in 1066 – they remember King Harold, the English hero who died with an arrow in his eye. But he was a man and a king, so he's remembered (even though he lost).

Sadly Jemima Nicholas (born in 1750) and the Pembroke Mum's Army have been almost forgotten. She was a woman, of course, and it doesn't seem to matter that she actually won. (You might have been reading this in French if she hadn't.)

Here are ten famous facts about her dramatic – and almost forgotten – story. Britain was at war with France and Admiral Nelson hadn't defeated them at sea (yet). So they set off to do just that.

1. On 22 February 1797, 1,500 French troops, known as the Black Legion, landed at Carreg Wastad, near Fishguard, on the west coast of Wales. The main French army was planning to invade Ireland and set it free from British rule.

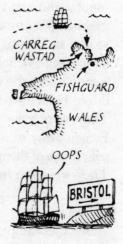

2. The French sent this force of 1,500 to attack Bristol – to make the English think THAT'S where the attack would be. But gales blew them past Bristol, so they sailed round to Fishguard.

3. The French expected the Welsh to rise up and fight with them against the English. Bad idea. But they picked a good place to land. The defenders only had eight cannons in the whole of Fishguard – and those cannons only had three cannonballs. So, what did the defenders do? They fired blanks. It kept the French quiet for hours till Lord Cawdor arrived with a proper army.

4. The French came ashore and found some barrels of wine that had been washed ashore the week before and they drank it all. There's a story that one Frenchman fell asleep in a farmhouse. He was so drunk he woke in the night and heard the click of a musket and fired at his enemy. It turned out to be the tick of a grandfather clock.

5. The local posh people grabbed their money and ran away. But the peasants grabbed pitchforks and scythes and even spades and joined Lord Cawdor's army.

6. Jemima Nicholas – a local cobbler – went out into the fields that day and saw a dozen French soldiers wandering around. They were poor soldiers – half of the French army were criminals fresh out of jails. Some of them still had ankle irons on. They were starving and drunk. Jemima caught them chasing her sheep and chickens to eat.

7. She picked up a pitchfork and pointed it at them. They threw down their weapons. Jemima marched them down to the local lock-up. She became a Welsh heroine and was awarded a pension of £50 a year for life.

8. Jemima and her friends joined Lord Cawdor's army to attack the rest of the French on the beach – just to see the sport really. They caught one or two French men on the way. One was bashed over the head with a chair leg, another was thrown down a well.

MON DIEU-
AGAIN

9. The French on the beach saw the women's red cloaks in the distance. They thought they were more redcoat soldiers coming to attack. They threw down their weapons.

YEE
HA?

10. That's how a Welsh woman helped to stop the last invasion of Britain. But the French army was led by an old American, Colonel Tate. The last invasion of Britain was American-led. Not a lot of people know that.

After this defeat the French never tried invading Britain again. In fact, no enemy has landed on Britain's shores since. (Unless you count a few German pilots shot down in the Second World War.)

I'M NOT INVADING, HONEST

See:
The Last Invasion Tapestry Gallery, Fishguard. A tapestry telling the story of Jemima Nicholas and the last French invasion.

Second World War – Dunkirk

The seas of Britain make it difficult for other nations to invade. But they also make it tricky to leave Britain and invade other countries.

At the start of the Second World War (1939–1945), Adolf Hitler's German army invaded France. Britain sent an army across the English Channel to help the French and drive the Germans back.

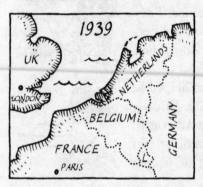 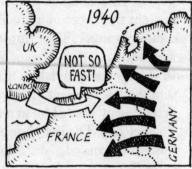

It was a bit of a disaster. It was the Germans who pushed the British army all the way back to the English Channel.

Now the British were trapped by the sea near the town of Dunkirk. The German army just had to move in and finish off the Brits.

The British Royal Navy had big warships and troop ships but they couldn't get very near to the beach to rescue the British troops. They needed 'little' boats.

The navy back in Britain searched the ports on the coast and found trading boats, fishing boats, pleasure craft, yachts, paddle steamers and lifeboats.

✹ The *Medway Queen* from Kent held the record with seven trips across the Channel and rescued 7,000 men. She was built to carry holiday families up and down the Rive Thames. She became known as the 'Heroine of Dunkirk'.

✹ The smallest boat was the fishing boat *Tamzine* whi was just 4.6 metres long.

✹ *Sundowner* was a motor yacht owned by Cha Lightoller. She was built to carry 21 passengers. She ca 127. Lightoller took a young sea-scout lived. Ch Lightoller had also been on th

...u 331,000 British and F

In nine   oy the 700 little ships and arou

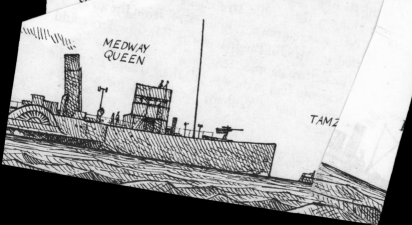

MEDWAY QUEEN

TAMZ

After the rescue at Dunkirk, the British prime minister, Winston Churchill, made a speech in which he said...

> We shall go on to the end. We shall fight in France, we shall fight on the seas and oceans, we shall defend our island, whatever the cost may be. We shall fight on the beaches, we shall fight on the landing grounds, we shall fight in the fields and in the streets, we shall fight in the hills; we shall never surrender.

Now the French coast had been captured by the German Army, they just had to cross the Channel and invade Britain.

Adolf Hitler came up with a plan called 'Operation Sea Lion'. After crushing the British and French at Dunkirk he said...

I HAVE DECIDED TO PREPARE A LANDING OPERATION AGAINST ENGLAND

The plans were made. The German soldiers along a forty-mile stretch of England. Maps were drawn, photos taken from 160,000 book printed with useful English words. The invader chat with the British people.

All the Germans had to do was sail their troops across the English Channel, just as William the Conqueror had done

900 years before. But William hadn't had the problem of being bombed by the Royal Air Force.

Hitler's orders said that first...

> THE RAF MUST BE BEATEN DOWN SO IT CAN NO LONGER ATTACK THE GERMAN CROSSING

The German air force – the Luftwaffe – set off to bomb British airfields. But they were shot down by the RAF fighter planes in an air-war known as the Battle of Britain.

Britain had been saved (again) by the English Channel, this time with the help of aeroplanes. Winston Churchill said the pilots were the bravest of the brave.

> NEVER WAS SO MUCH OWED BY SO MANY TO SO FEW

The fightback
After five years of war the German armies were being defeated. It was time for Britain to set sail from France again. This time with the help of US forces.

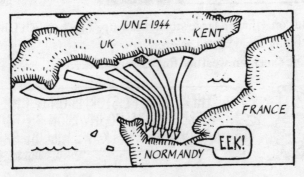

The plan was called 'Operation Overlord'. Now it's remembered as D-Day – the Day of Days.

First the British and Americans tricked the Germans into thinking they were going to attack Norway – they sent fake radio messages saying that.

Then they pretended the invasion would start in Kent – they placed dummy tanks in fields there so a German spotter plane would think they were real tanks. The real invasion was going to set off from west of there.

Then they had practice landings. They couldn't land on the French beaches, obviously. But beaches in Devon were very similar. The poor people of Slapton in Devon were told to leave their houses for many months while the armies practised.

By June everything was ready ... except the weather. The thing that had wrecked the Armada. The American commander, General Eisenhower, said...

I WANT TO START THE ATTACK ON 5 JUNE. THE TIDES ARE RIGHT AND THERE WILL BE A FULL MOON

But on 4 June a large storm blew up. The English Channel was being as awkward as ever.

The German weather forecasters said...

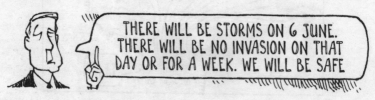

THERE WILL BE STORMS ON 6 JUNE. THERE WILL BE NO INVASION ON THAT DAY OR FOR A WEEK. WE WILL BE SAFE

Now the British were trapped by the sea near the town of Dunkirk. The German army just had to move in and finish off the Brits.

The British Royal Navy had big warships and troop ships but they couldn't get very near to the beach to rescue the British troops. They needed 'little' boats.

The navy back in Britain searched the ports on the coast and found trading boats, fishing boats, pleasure craft, yachts, paddle steamers and lifeboats.

* The *Medway Queen* from Kent held the record with seven trips across the Channel and rescued 7,000 men. She was built to carry holiday families up and down the River Thames. She became known as the 'Heroine of Dunkirk'.

* The smallest boat was the fishing boat *Tamzine* which was just 4.6 metres long.

* *Sundowner* was a motor yacht owned by Charles Lightoller. She was built to carry 21 passengers. She carried 127. Lightoller took a young sea-scout to help. Charles Lightoller had also been on the *Titanic* and lived.

In nine days, more than 331,000 British and French soldiers were rescued by the 700 little ships and around 220 warships.

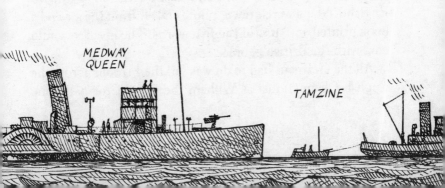

MEDWAY
QUEEN

TAMZINE

After the rescue at Dunkirk, the British prime minister, Winston Churchill, made a speech in which he said...

> *We shall go on to the end. We shall fight in France, we shall fight on the seas and oceans, we shall defend our island, whatever the cost may be. We shall fight on the beaches, we shall fight on the landing grounds, we shall fight in the fields and in the streets, we shall fight in the hills; we shall never surrender.*

Now the French coast had been captured by the German Army, they just had to cross the Channel and invade Britain.

Adolf Hitler came up with a plan called 'Operation Sea Lion'. After crushing the British and French at Dunkirk he said...

I HAVE DECIDED TO PREPARE A LANDING OPERATION AGAINST ENGLAND

The plans were made. The Germans would land 160,000 soldiers along a forty-mile stretch of coast in southeast England. Maps were drawn, photos taken from the air and a book printed with useful English words. The invaders could chat with the British people.

All the Germans had to do was sail their troops across the English Channel, just as William the Conqueror had done

...so many German troops went on holiday. A British weather forecaster (Group Captain James Stagg of the Royal Air Force) said...

> 6 JUNE WILL BE GOOD. I THINK YOU SHOULD INVADE THEN

But who was right?

More than 5,000 vessels set off from the south coast of England.

James Stagg had been right after all. The English Channel weather behaved itself. The invasion went ahead. Nearly 160,000 troops crossed the English Channel on 6 June 1944, and more than two million Allied troops were in France by the end of August.

By 1945 the German army had surrendered.

See:

1. The *Medway Queen* at Gillingham Pier. In 1963 she was sent to be scrapped in Belgium. When the scrap yard found she was the 'Heroine of Dunkirk' they refused. She was saved and rebuilt.
2. The fishing boat *Tamzine* at the Imperial War Museum in London.
3. *Sundowner* is in Ramsgate Maritime Museum.

> IT'S NICE NOBODY'S SHOOTING AT US ANYMORE

Scott and his team sailed south in June 1910. They discovered that a Norwegian team, led by Roald Amundsen, had set off before them. They could still win, but it would be a race.

By December 1910 the ship was hit by a heavy storm. The ship began to leak and the pumps failed. The crew had to bail her out with buckets. Scott lost two ponies and a dog in the storm.

Lawrence Oates was meant to buy special ponies for the trip, but he was late joining the team. Someone else had to buy them and they turned out to be useless.

He planned to use petrol-driven sledges too, but one of the sleds fell through the ice as it was being unloaded in Antarctica and was lost in the sea. The others kept breaking down.

In September 1911, Scott explained his plans for the South Pole march. Sixteen men would set out, using the two remaining motor sledges, ponies and dogs. When they reached the Beardmore Glacier, the dogs would return to base.

Lawrence Oates, in charge of the ponies, told Scott to kill the weaker ponies for dog food. Scott refused to do this.

Scott was al...
was written on...

It seen
I can
look

The bodies o...
by a search par...

It seems he...
Scott's group o...
being used tod...

See:
The Scott Polar Res...
Museum open to the...
is also shown there,

Oates told Scott, 'You'll be sorry' ... in the end they were BOTH sorry. Four ponies died on this journey either from the cold or because they slowed the team down and had to be shot. Three fell through the ice.

Scott and four of the team reached the pole on 17 January 1912. They were horrified to find Roald Amundsen's Norwegian team had beaten them by five weeks.

It is said that Amundsen left a note in his tent for Scott to find...

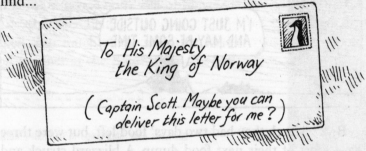

To His Majesty
the King of Norway

(Captain Scott. Maybe you can
deliver this letter for me?)

That was Amundsen gloating. Cruel.

Scott turned for home. His team set off to meet the dog sleds with new supplies. But the man in charge of bringing the dogs was too busy waiting for a ship to take him home. The weather grew worse. In the end no one took the dogs and supplies to the meeting point.

One by one Scott's team of four died. On 17 February, Scott found Edgar Evans, and wrote...

The poor man was on his knees with
hands uncovered and frostbitten, and
a wild look in his eyes.

Evans died that night.

Lawrence ...
could hardly ...
side. It mea...
freeze and k...
Scott refuse...
a blizzard, t...
could move ...
to Scott wer...

By 22 Ma... they ...
days short o... their way ...
stopped them moving a...
again. Wilson wrote to ... Oriana ...

Bowers wrote ...

Superstitions

Sailing wooden ships across stormy seas was a dangerous business. A metre to the starboard and you'll hit a rock, sink and die. With luck you'll miss that rock.

Lucky for sailors

Sailors believed in luck ... and there were some things that brought good luck and some that brought bad luck. So, before you set off in your canoe, just remember the rules...

For GOOD luck...

BING BONG

1 Sail on a Sunday ... but never the first Monday of April

2 Bring a 'ship's cat' as it will bring your boat good luck

3 Get a tattoo with a good luck sign

4 Pour wine on deck as you set sail

5 Step on the ship with your right foot first

6 Smash your eggshells to pieces

7 Spot an albatross

8 Wear a gold earring to save you from drowning

9 Place a lucky coin under a ship's mast when it is raised

10 Don't take a man called Jonah on your crew

Sea several weeks before. At last, word reached him. Bad news. A terrible storm had battered Anne's fleet and many sailors' lives had been lost.

James decided to set sail from Edinburgh to Denmark to collect his Anne. No sooner had his ship entered the North Sea than terrible storms forced his captain to turn back.

Someone seemed out to get him and James knew who to blame. Scottish witches. He was sure witches from North Berwick were out to kill him. He had heard the stories. Gossips said that one witch had sailed into the Firth of Forth, on a sieve, to call up the storm.

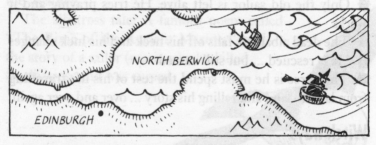

Just to the east of Edinburgh there is the small town of North Berwick. People told James there were around 70 witches in that small place. James was told the witches met at St Andrew's Church. It was on the seafront and looked out to where the storm hit his ship. Perfect for the witches, he said.

He sent his officers to arrest the people of North Berwick. In England, at that time, witches were hanged. In Scotland they were burned alive. So, of course, the men and women said...

NOT GUILTY

James was sure they were lying. All he had to do was have the witches tortured and they would own up.

His torturers used a few different ways of bringing terrible pain to the poor people. Can you match the name of the torture device to the way it was used? They used...

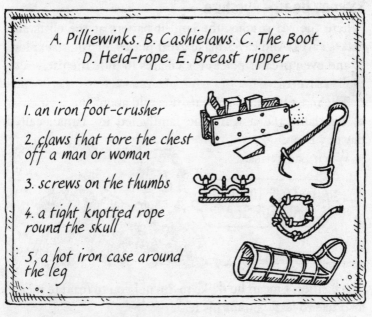

A. Pilliewinks. B. Cashielaws. C. The Boot.
D. Heid-rope. E. Breast ripper

1. an iron foot-crusher

2. claws that tore the chest off a man or woman

3. screws on the thumbs

4. a tight knotted rope round the skull

5. a hot iron case around the leg

Answers: A – 3 B – 5 C – 1 D – 4 E – 2

In the torture room people like Gellie Duncan now said...

WE DUG CORPSES FROM THE GRAVEYARDS, TOOK THEM APART, TIED THE LIMBS TO DEAD CATS AND THEN THREW THE WHOLE LOT INTO THE SEA TO MAKE A STORM TO KILL THE KING

Of course, that is nonsense and it won't work (so don't try

it). But they said it just to stop the pain. Gellie was tied to a stake and burned alive.

Memorials to the dead people can still be found in the North Berwick graveyard today.

Sawney Bean – Ayrshire

Where the sea reaches the land it batters at the cliffs and makes caves. And caves make great places for you to explore ... and even greater places for villains to hide themselves or their treasures.

The most horrible cave tale was told about the west coast of Scotland and a fearsome family led by a man called Sawney Bean.

When Sawney said...

I'D LOVE TO HAVE YOU FOR TEA

...he didn't mean he'd like to 'invite' you to tea. He meant he'd like to 'eat' you for his tea.

The story goes that this cruel cannibal was born in East Lothian (close to Edinburgh) around the 1200s or 1300s. Sawney hated his farm job in East Lothian so he ran away with his new wife to live in a cave on the beach in Galloway.

How did they survive on this bleak and windswept coast by the chilly Irish Sea? By fishing? Hard work for idle Sawney. He had a much better idea. For 25 years he and his family robbed and murdered travellers on the Ayrshire roads.

But they were a long way from shops.

So, what do you think they ate? They ate their murder victims. They munched their way through about one person a week. If the family couldn't manage a whole man for dinner then they hung up the leftovers in the cave. A smoky fire stopped them going off.

The law sent in the army to catch the highway robbers but they never found Sawney's cave hideouts. Over the years innocent people were arrested and executed for his crimes. The Bean family were careful never to let anyone escape to give away their secrets. Then, one evening, a gang of young Beans leapt out on a husband and wife who were on horseback. The poor wife was dragged to the ground, her throat was cut and the Beans drank her blood. Just as they were about to carry her off a gang of horsemen arrived, and the horrified husband was able to escape.

When the husband returned to the coast he had an army of 400 of the King's men. The Beans were hunted down and arrested. They were taken to Edinburgh for execution. The king decided not to waste time with a trial. Now we get to the really nasty bit… not thinking about dinner, are you?

And there you have it … a clan of baked Beans.
A popular poem of 200 years ago told their grim tale…

THEY HUNG THEM HIGH IN EDINBURGH TOWN
AND LIKEWISE, ALL THEIR KIN.
AND THE WIND BLOWS COLD UPON
THEIR BONES.
AND TO HELL THEY ALL HAVE GONE

A horrible story. But the good news is, it is just a legend.

YES, there were probably robbers on the Galloway coast. BUT the cannibal family who escaped for 25 years is nonsense.

And there are no records of such bloody executions in Edinburgh – ever. It was supposed to have happened at the Tolbooth Prison – but the Tolbooth wasn't even built in the 1300s – it was built in 1561.

So, it's safe to swim on the Galloway beaches. Sawney Bean will not be seen.

Flannan Isle mystery – Ross-shire and Cromartyshire

Winter winds bring wild weather – tempests to towns, hurricanes to houses, sleet to cities and gales to gardens. Winds that whip wild waves at sea bring wrecks and ruin to struggling ships.

Lighthouse keepers

Lighthouse keepers were the brave blokes out there who sat alone in tall towers keeping brilliant bulbs blinking to steer ships away from razor rocks.

They were the men who manned lighthouses around the coasts. They saved countless lives. But one January night it was the keepers who suffered in one of the spookiest history mysteries of all time.

THE HEBRIDES HERALD

29 December 1900

 A GANNET STOLE MY WHISKEY – FULL STORY INSIDE

LIGHTHOUSE HORROR

Fear has come to the Flannan Isles where three lighthouse keepers seem to have vanished from the face of the earth. Lighthouse inspector Robert Muirhead visited the island today looking for answers – and looking for the three missing men. He found no answers. No men.

'I know they were there on 15 December,' he told our reporter. 'The lighthouse light was out on 15 December. We know that. But a ship couldn't get to the island until Boxing Day to see what was wrong.'

What did the crew of the Boxing Day ship find? 'There was no flag on the flagpole,' Muirhead reported, 'no food boxes waiting to be filled and no lighthouse keepers rowing out to meet the boat.'

Joe Moore rowed ashore and went to the keepers' house to find out where they were. The doors were all locked, their beds had been slept in and the clock had stopped. There had been a set of oilskin coats to shelter the men from the worst of the weather. There was just one coat there. Muirhead said, 'It looks as if one man had gone out without a coat. In the December storms he must have been crazy to go out without a coat.'

Joe Moore found the lighthouse lamps were cleaned and filled with oil, ready to light. A chair in the kitchen had been knocked over. The man searched the island and there was not another person to be found.

He reported back to the ship and the captain sent a message to the mainland: 'Poor fellows must have been blown over the cliffs or drowned or something like that.'

Mr Muirhead said, 'There was terrible damage on the landing stage. The storm had ripped and twisted iron railings, washed away a storehouse and thrown huge crates around. I believe the men went to try and rescue the crates but were washed away by a mammoth wave.'

That sounds sensible but people in the Oban Inn have their own ideas about what happened.

Mrs Kilwellie from the post office said, 'My Archie says one keeper murdered the other two and felt so guilty he threw himself into the sea.'

Her neighbour, Mrs McKay, argued, 'We've heard about the monster of Loch Ness. Well, there are bigger monsters out at sea. It was a monster that carried them off.'

'Or a huge bird,' her husband said.

'The men were missing their women,' Ellen Bruce said. 'When they saw a mermaid they ran into the sea to catch her and she drowned them. That's what mermaids do for sport.'

'Nonsense and fairy tales,' the innkeeper said. 'There are German spies all around. The keepers saw a German warship off the coast, doing things it shouldn't. The Germans landed and shot them to keep them quiet.'

The Oban Police sergeant, Peter Blackwell, scoffed at these ideas. 'Everyone has heard ghost stories of the Flannan Phantom. Take my word for it, an evil spirit made the men terrified. There was nowhere to run so they threw themselves off the cliffs.'

Inspector Robert Muirhead said, 'The fact is we may never know the truth.'

But so long as no one knows what happened the people of the Hebrides will walk the shores in fear of monsters and ghosts, birds and waves.

Missing lighthouse keepers

This mystery has never been solved. Some people think the keepers were snatched by aliens from outer space. There have been songs and poems and books about the mystery. There has even been a *Doctor Who* episode about it.

A poet wrote as if he was one of the men who landed and found an empty island…

Yet, as we crowded through the door,
We only saw a table, spread
For dinner, meat and cheese and bread;
But, all untouched; and no one there,
As though, when they sat down to eat,
Ere they could even taste,
Alarm had come, and they in haste
Had risen and left the bread and meat,
For at the table head a chair
Lay tumbled on the floor.

Spooky … but wrong. There was NO meal on the table. Someone had tidied the kitchen up before disaster struck.

If you believe in aliens then you may think it was a very tidy little green man from Mars.

If you don't believe in aliens, then it will stay a mystery. Unless you can solve it?

'John the Jibber' – Durham

All along the North Durham coast there are cliffs with deep caves. The nearest big towns are five miles away, so in days long gone they were dark. A great place, perfect for smugglers to land their cargo.

The big ships dropped the secret supplies into rowing boats and the smugglers rowed them to the shore. They didn't want to leave the precious rum and tobacco, sugar and tea on the beach. The barrels and boxes could be hidden in the caves.

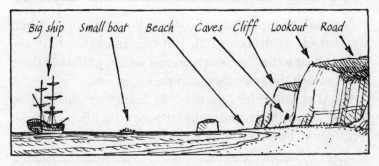

Big ship   Small boat   Beach   Caves   Cliff   Lookout   Road

Then, when the smugglers were ready, they could lower ropes from the cliff-top and haul up their precious stuff. The deep caves are still there today, and the biggest one is known as Marsden Grotto.

In 1782 Jack Bates and his wife, Jessie, set out in the smuggling trade at Marsden. Jack borrowed explosives from a local quarry. Jack and Jessie blasted a small cave into a much larger one – the Grotto. The local people called him 'Jack the Blaster'.

123

Jack then set about building a zig-zag stairway down the cliff and set up home in the Grotto. This odd choice of house had visitors. Those visitors were given drinks – which they paid for. It was an illegal pub.

Most of those visitors were smugglers.

SMUGGLERS? NEVER. THEY TOLD ME THEY WERE FISHERMEN

Jack hid their supplies in his deep cave, and they gave him free barrels of drink to sell. But one smuggler, John the Jibber, went to the customs men and said he could tell them how to catch the smugglers ... if they paid him.

But the smugglers escaped by dumping their cargo further down the coast at a lighthouse called Souter Point. They found out it was John the Jibber who'd betrayed them.

I ALWAYS SAID THAT JIBBER WAS A FIBBER

When the smugglers found John the Jibber they hung him in a barrel, inside a shaft cal'ed the Smuggler's Hole. It was just along the cliff-side from Marsden Grotto. The Jibber was left to starve to death.

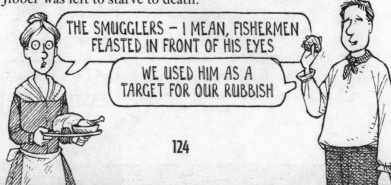

THE SMUGGLERS – I MEAN, FISHERMEN FEASTED IN FRONT OF HIS EYES

WE USED HIM AS A TARGET FOR OUR RUBBISH

And now, it is said, on dark, stormy nights, the Jibber's ghostly wails can be heard above the sound of the howling winds.

Go to Marsden Grotto – it's still a pub built into a cave – and, as you feast on steak and sticky toffee pudding, you may hear his sad, sad cries...

See:
Marsden Grotto, South Shields, and the caves along the beach.

Sea monsters

If you were a sailor, and you came home, what could you tell people about your trip?

It's no surprise that sailors came up with the most incredible stories to tell their friends and families. Stories about fantastic sea beasts that they said they met in the deep, dark depths...

1. Morgawr

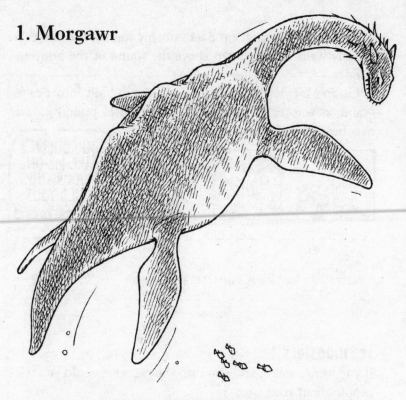

In 1976 Mrs Scott of Falmouth, Cornwall, reported a long-necked, hump-backed monster off the coast.

But this was not the first sighting. This creature seems to appear every 50 years. Back in 1876 a newspaper reported...

🗼 WEST BRITON NEWSPAPER ⛵

MEN SEE MONSTER

A sea serpent has been caught alive in Gerrans Bay. Two of our fishermen were checking their crab pots around a quarter mile from shore. They discovered a serpent coiled around the buoy. As they drew near it raised its head as if to attack so they struck it hard with their oars. It was stunned and that let them get on with their work. Soon after it was dashed against the rocks and drifted back out to sea. Local people call it a Morgawr.

---

50 years later another Morgawr was spotted on the same part of the coast.

If they appear every 50 years then the next one is due in 2026. Be ready to defend yourself like those crab fishers.

OARSOME!

I HOPE I DON'T GET OAR-STRUCK!

2. Qalupalik

Everyone has heard of mermaids – creatures who are human above the waist and fish below. In the children's tale *The Little Mermaid*, the mermaid falls in love with a human prince and comes to an unhappy end.

But sailors' legends are of far nastier creatures. The Qalupalik they met in North America has green skin, razor-sharp teeth and long, grasping fingernails. Nastiest of all, the Qalupalik likes to kidnap children playing near the shore. It uses a humming voice to lure them to the edge of the water.

Just remember, the poor Qalupalik needs to munch young human flesh to stay young itself. Maybe let it have a finger or a toe you hardly ever use?

3. Leviathan

This brutal beast is unstoppable. So, if you are sunbathing on the beach and see one, don't even bother trying to escape. It is a fire-breathing sea monster that will boil the water around you. That'll cook your flesh nicely for when it chews on your chops.

The Leviathan is described in four parts of the Bible. It's savage and a creature of the Devil that has existed since the mists of time. The problem (the Bible says) is that just the look of the twisted monster can scare you to death...

ONE SHALL BE CAST DOWN EVEN AT THE SIGHT OF HIM.

Apparently, only God can defeat the Leviathan. So, start saying prayers if you see one rising from the deep fat fryer in your local chip shop.

OH MY GOD!

4. Finfolk

The seas off the Orkney Isles in Scotland are the home of the Finfolk – a gang of evil fishy wizards. The trouble is they can change shape and appear like normal humans. (My maths teacher was one of them.)

Finfolk, looking human, can enter your seaside town and kidnap men and women. The victims are dragged off to underwater palaces with crystal halls. Sounds nice? No, the humans are forced to marry a Finfolk and be their slave.

But there IS an escape. Throw silver coins on the ground – the Finfolk will grasp at the silver that they love – then make a run for it.

5. Cirein-croin

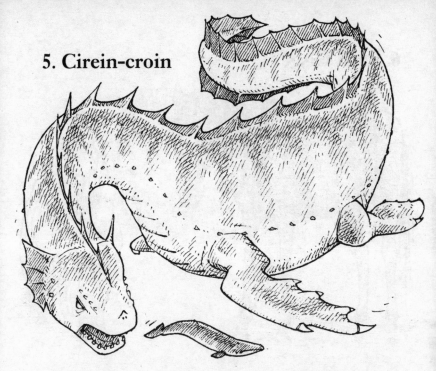

Another Scottish sea monster. This one is so large it tucks into seven whales for dinner. But its greatest trick is to shrink down to the size of your hand.

A fisherman can catch this hand-sized creature. As soon as it lands on the deck of his boat the monster expands back to its full size. It then swallows the fisherman whole.

If you meet one on your seaside holiday you could try offering it some food...

WHY DON'T YOU HAVE MY ANNOYING LITTLE BROTHER INSTEAD OF ME?

URGH! NO THANKS

6. Each Uisge

And yet another Scottish sea horror. This one is a water-horse. But it can disguise itself as a lovely pony and invite you to have a pleasant little ride. Don't. As soon as you sit on it, the skin sticks to you like glue and it heads back to its home beneath the sea, taking you with it. Can you breathe underwater? If not then you'll drown.

Your body will be torn apart and the only bit the Each Uisge leaves is your liver. That is left to float to the surface.

EPILOGUE

The seas around the British Isles have made Britain what it is. And it has made the British people what they are...

🏵 Sailors ... from great battleships like Nelson's *Victory* to the tiny fishing boat *Tamzine* from a seaside town of Margate
🏵 Heroes ... like Grace Darling and Jack Crawford
🏵 Villains ... like Blackbeard and the slave traders
🏵 Explorers ... from Drake, the first captain to sail around the world, to Captain Robert Scott, who died trying to conquer the Antarctic.

What it has given YOU are some fabulous stories. Some of them - like the disaster of *Rothsay Castle* - are horrible. Some – like the race between the little *Sirius* and the mighty *Great Western* – are as exciting as any adventure story.

So, next time you see the sea, say, 'Thank you.' It's given us some remarkable tales that should live forever.

INDEX

Also available

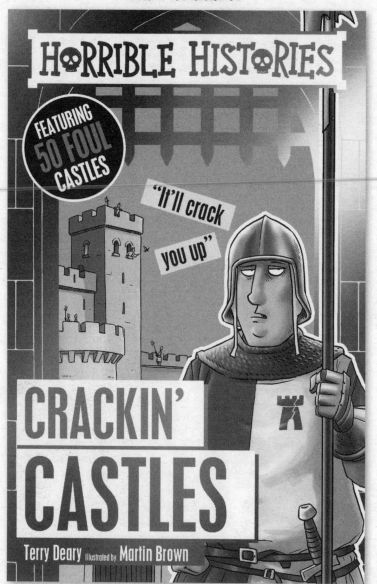

HORRIBLE HISTORIES

"It's ruff at the top."

TOP 50
KINGS & QUEENS

Terry Deary Illustrated by Martin Brown

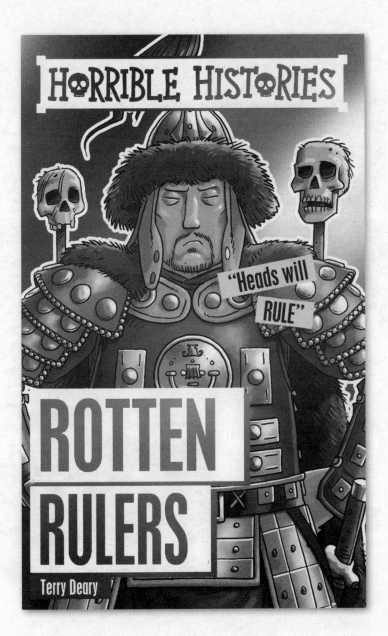

HORRIBLE HISTORIES

"Heads will RULE"

ROTTEN
RULERS

Terry Deary

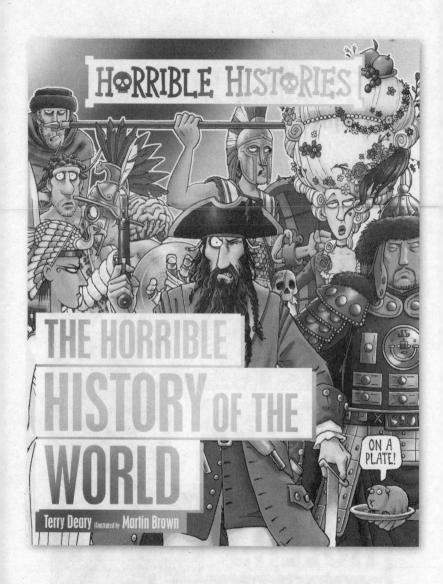

HORRIBLE HISTORIES

THE HORRIBLE HISTORY OF THE WORLD

ON A PLATE!

Terry Deary Illustrated by Martin Brown

It's HISTORY with the NASTY bits left in!